TRADITIONAL SOUTH... ITALIAN MANDOLIN & FIDDLE TUNES

by John T. La Barbera

Online Audio   www.melbay.com/21488BCDEB

Audio Contents

1	Abballati, Abballati	13	Fronni d'Alia	25	Pizzicarella
2	Alla Carpinese	14	Il Ritornello delle Lavandaie del Vomero	26	Ricciulina
3	Alziti Bbella	15	La `Ndrezzata	27	Serenata Amalfitana
4	Angelare`	16	La Palumella	28	Sonos `E Memoria
5	Antidotum Tarantulae (part 1)	17	La Procidana	29	Tammurriata
6	Antidotum Tarantulae (part 2)	18	La Sant'Allegrezza	30	Tarantella "Nfuocata
7	Bo e la ri-bo`	19	La Zita Passa	31	Tarantella di Ogliastro
8	Cu Ti Lu Dissi	20	Marenaresca	32	Tarantella dell'600
9	Danza Siciliana	21	Matajola	33	Tarantella Paesana
10	Fasola Siciliana	22	Motivo di Cantastorie	34	Villanella Ch'all'Aqua Vai
11	Figghia di'n Massaru	23	Pizzicarella Mia	35	Volumbrella
12	Fischiettando	24	Pizzica-Pizzica	36	Vurria Addeventare

Audio Engineer: Joe Stavitsky

1 2 3 4 5 6 7 8 9 0

Visit us on the Web at www.melbay.com   E-mail us at email@melbay.com

This book is dedicated to my son, Sebastian,
who has the spirit of a real *Giullari*.

Acknowledgements

Photo Credits: David Blazer, Colita, Barcelona (Spagna), Pier Paulo Alberti, M.B.Lapin

Compiled, transcribed and edited by: John T. LaBarbera
Arrangements by: John T. La Barbera

Special Thanks to:
All of my friends from the music and theater company **Pupi e Fresedde,** who were very patient, treated me as a
brother from L'America and who inspired and brought me into the world of this music: Pino de Vittorio, Fulvio
Sebastio, Gianni Castellana, Luciano Vavolo, Tomasella Calvisi, Alfio Antico and the director of the company
Angelo Savelli, at Teatro Rifreddi, in Florence, Italy; the late Sardinian folk singer, Maria Carta; Dr. David
Blazer, my witness with this musical experience on both sides of the Atlantic; Alessandra Belloni, co-founder,
singer -percussionist of I Giullari di Piazza who shared promoting this music with me in the U.S. since 1979;
Dr. Joseph Scelsa from the Italian American Museum in New York City; Dr. Joseph Sciorra, The John D. Ca-
landra Italian American Institute (Queens College, CUNY); Anna Lomax Wood; The Very Reverend James
Parks Morton, former Dean of the Cathedral of St. John the Divine, NYC; and especially both my parents
Thomas and Helen La Barbera, who always supported my music and taught me to pursue my dreams.

Table of Contents

Music

Introduction

This book is in part a method book, not exactly for beginners, that includes some traditional techniques which might be new to mandolinist already familiar with the instrument. It is also a collection of traditional southern Italian folk music. Whether you play flat back or bowl back Neapolitan mandolin, violin, or just interested in Italian folk music, this book will further your interest in the music from this rich tradition. Both the mandolin and the violin share a common bond together in Italian music in both the classical and folk traditions. The association of the mandolin with the standard Neapolitan songs of the late 1800's up until the middle of the twentieth century has certainly reached worldwide acclaim. Throughout the development of the mandolin there exists printed manuscripts and scores for the repertoire of the instrument as well as method books dating back to the eighteenth and early nineteenth centuries. The classical mandolin has a very good supply of printed music from Vivaldi to Beethoven, as well as the repertoire from the mandolin virtuosi who toured concert halls all over the world from the 1800's thru the twentieth century. Many historical references dating back as far as the sixteenth century, speak of the popular music played by street musicians with mandolins and guitars. You might wonder what some of that music sounded like. This book presents some of that music for the first time.

It is not surprising that relatively very little is known about this vast repertoire. Probably one of the first sources of preserving folk music in Italy is attributed to a 17th century Jesuit alchemist, Athanasius Kircher (1601-1680), who transcribed some of the tarantellas that were being played for the cure of an illness caused by the sting of the tarantula. During the late 1800's, the musicologist-composer, Alberto Favara, set out to transcribe traditional folk music of his native Sicily. He published *Canti Popolari Siciliani*, in 1921.

As late as the 1950's and early 1960's, traditional music was only heard in small villages and only for rituals, working in the fields, or feasts in honor of the Madonna and Saints. Fortunately, during the 1950's, musicologists Diego Carpitella and Alan Lomax traveled throughout Italy making field recordings of the music from remote areas and inspired many others to continue. Their work was extremely valuable in preserving the authentic styles. In my estimation some of the songs played by the roving street musicians in large cities such as Rome and Naples, were songs popular from the country side. It is very difficult to say when some of these songs originated.

According to Alan Lomax, Italy has the most complete folk song history in Western Europe which dates back to pre-Christian Roman and Greco influences. Many customs from these times are still evident in the remote areas

During a performance of *Sulla Via di San Michele*
with Pupi e Fresedde (1978-Florence)
Luciano Vavolo, Tomasella Calvisi,
John La Barbera (chitarra battente),
Fulvio Sebastio, and Patricia De Libero.

of southern Italy. As Lomax discovered in the 1950's, traces of every period in Italian history could still be heard in the folk music. The songs that have survived clearly have passed the test of time. Some of the songs such as the *"Antidotum Tarantulae"* and the Neapolitan villanelle we know are from the 1600's and have the characteristics of renaissance music.

I was very fortunate to have learned many of these songs while living in Italy during the early 1970's, when there was a resurgence of interest in traditional music. At that time, the Neapolitan composer and director Roberto De Simone and his group, *La Nuova Compagnia di Canto Popolare,* had led the way by performing and recording songs from the region of Naples. With new arrangements he brought forward many unknown traditional songs based on his research. Many of the tunes in this book were taught to me as I sat down with my guitar and mandolin in an apartment in Florence with the street musicians who later formed the musical group *Pupi e Fresedde.* They were all from the south of Italy and began singing their traditional songs on the streets and piazzas of Florence, just as it might have been in the sixteenth century. Joining their original troupe and performing and touring with them all over Europe and on the east coast of the United States for several years, I began to realize the vast repertoire of songs that existed and how much of it had been past down by oral tradition. It also gave me an excellent opportunity to be part of the tradition itself and inspired me to continue researching more about this music as well as understanding how it was to be played with the right feeling and gusto.

Upon my arrival back to the United States in 1979, I had felt so enriched by the experiences I had in Italy performing and recording with *Pupi e Fresedde* on the album *La Terra Del Rimorso* (Divergo-Polygram, DVAP 029), that I wanted to bring to American audiences these beautiful melodies and rhythms. (I was sure that my Italian grandparents would have been proud of me). Also for the Italian-American community, I felt it was important to re-connect this music that many had forgotten upon their arrival in the new world. That year, I formed the group *I Giullari di Piazza* in New York City, (my home town) together with the Italian actor Claudio Saponi, from Rimini, who was a highly trained actor in Italian theater especially the *Commedia del'Arte*, and with Alessandra Belloni from Rome, Italy. With all of the music I had learned in Italy, I began to teach musicians this repertoire while making my own arrangements as well as writing new compositions inspired on the traditional forms. At first the American audiences were not accustomed to this kind of Italian music and most people wanted us to play the standard Italian music that had already been absorbed into the mainstream. The Tarantella was only known as an Italian wedding dance and no one had ever heard of a Pizzica or Tammurriata. However, the musicians that I first started to teach this music to were very supportive

Maria Carta
photo: Colita, Barcellona (Spagna)

and eager to learn all about the music and traditions connected to it. During the early 1980's the group *I Giullari di Piazza* were beginning to make these songs heard to new audiences in New York and throughout the States, presented in theatrical productions which included music, theater and dance. In 1986, I had the great opportunity to work together and tour with one of the most famous singers of traditional Sardinian music, Maria Carta. Known throughout the world for her haunting and heart felt interpretation of Sardinian music she had often been described as Italy's Joan Baez. I had already been familiar with the unique guitar playing style while living in Italy, however working with her on a tour of just voice and guitar forced me to pay close attention to the fine articulation necessary for Sardinian music. She had also taught me so many beautiful songs during our rehearsals, that I cherish them like precious little jewels.

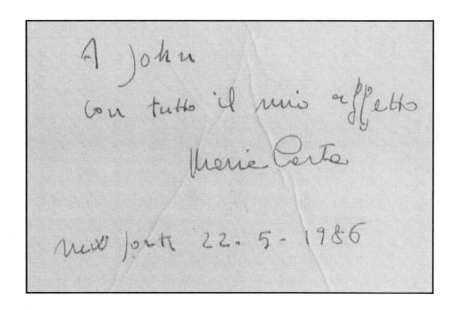

Many of the pieces in this book started out on scrapes of paper that I had made while transcribing the music that was sung to me by my friends while I lived in Italy. I have kept these pieces very dear to me for many years and I know that they will continue to inspire those who will hear them for the first time. The purpose of this book is to give tribute to some of these songs and dances from the southern Italian folk tradition.

John T. La Barbera

I Giullari di Piazza
Southern Italian Music, Theater and Dance (est. 1979)
Left to right: Carnivale Puppet (Dario Bollini), Susan Eberenz, Abram Stuart,
Alessandra Belloni, Enrico Granafei, John T. La Barbera and Ivan Thomas

About the Mandolin

The Neapolitan Mandolin, also known as the round back or bowled back mandolin, may have descended from the tenth century when similar instruments such as the Ud were first introduced through Arabic culture in Southern Italy. Throughout medieval and renaissance Europe, these instruments evolved and developed their own unique playing styles and various terms were used to describe them such as: lute, quintern, chitarra, and pandora. An instrument referred to as the *mandola* first appeared in Italian documents in Florence in the late sixteenth century. Manuscripts about the Italian *Commedia dell'Arte* also referred to it as an instrument used by 'Scappino', one of it's stock comic characters and the most musical of the *Commedia* troupe. Even the great violin maker, Antonio Stradivari, was also responsible for making an instrument called the mandolino, however at that time the instrument had five courses and gut strings and could be considered a soprano lute.

By the sixteenth century, Naples was the cultural capital of Southern Italy and its style of music and instruments influenced all of Europe. The use of metal strung, plectrum instruments had already been popular in Naples with instruments such as the colascione and the chitarra battente and were used to accompany popular songs and dances. It was not until the major developments in construction made by Neapolitan luthiers in the eighteenth and nineteenth century, that the mandolin continued to be successful. One of these first important luthiers was Gaetano Vinaccia whose instruments were widely in use during the 1740's. However, his son Pasquale, could be credited for redesigning a mandolin around the 1830's which used eight metal strings, or four courses, was played with a plectrum made of tortoiseshell instead of a quill and was tuned in fifths, (g,d,a,e) similar to the violin.

Because the mandolin was now fitted with steel strings, an influence that might have come from new innovations on the piano and violin, Vinaccia also changed the construction of the instrument in order to fit the tension of the strings and to produce more volume. Thus, the modern mandolin was born. The instrument became known as the Neapolitan Mandolin especially because of its popularity in and around Naples and it's success was quickly influencing the rest of the world.

By the late 1800's, mandolins were very much in demand and with the rise of Italian immigration to America, mandolins were being manufactured in the United States. Italian luthiers were working for larger manufacturers such as Lyon and Healy of Chicago and the C.F. Martin company in Nazareth, Pennsylvania. Some of these luthiers tried to work on their own and set up shops in downtown New York City where the Italian population was the greatest. One of them was Angelo Mannello, who emigrated to New York from Naples in 1885.

The standard Neapolitan design had not changed much since Vinaccia until 1898 when Orville Gibson, an inventor from upstate New York, came up with a successful design of a mandolin with a flat back. The idea of a flat back had been unsuccessful before and not very popular. Gibson finally got his patent in 1902 and the flat back mandolin began to flourish and seep into the mainstream of American music.

There have been many debates since that time over the preference and sound of the two instruments. Whatever your preference, you will find the music in this book to be very rewarding as you enjoy playing authentic tunes from Southern Italy.

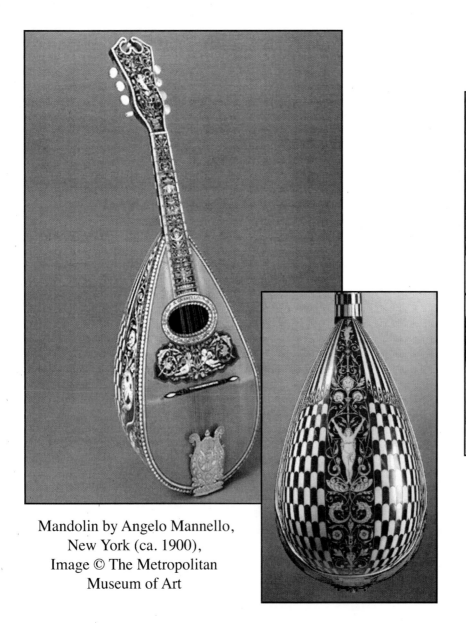

Mandolin by Angelo Mannello,
New York (ca. 1900),
Image © The Metropolitan
Museum of Art

The Barber Shop Quartet:
Guitar and Mandolin was always the
Barber's instrument of choice.
Giuseppe Scelsa (front row, left) was
part of a musical quartet in this shop on
the Lower East Side of Manhattan.

The Giuseppe Scelsa guitar and mandolin duo.
Early 20th Century New York

Styles of Traditional Music

Throughout all of Italy, from the north to the south, the folk music of each region has it's own particular style that distinguishes them apart. I have dedicated this book solely to the regions of southern Italy (including Rome), Naples, Calabria, Basilicata, Puglia and Sicily. Some of the styles are:

Love Songs: Usually in slow 2/4 or 4/4 time. Love songs also appear as serenades or ballads such as, "Alziti Bella."

Narrative Song: In various rhythms. These songs are about true events and tell stories. They are also known as ballads. Songs like "Fronni d'Alia" or "Figgia di'n Massaru" tell sensational stories of love and death. Many of these songs were originally passed down by roaming balladers or storytellers and later passed down to laborers who sang them as work songs to pass the time away.

Serenades: Originally were played from sunset on, ("*sera*" which means evening) and were usually courtship songs played to one's beloved or for devotional reasons as to pay one's respect. The fisherman serenades are mostly in 6/8 or 9/8 time and have a very calming quality to them for example: "La Procidana." There is also the "Mattinata", which were performed after midnight until sunrise. They were mostly devotional songs for saints or the Madonna.

Tarantella: The dance of the south, is found in 6/8, 9/8 and 12/8 time. Not all tarantellas are fast. Some are in 4/4 and begin in a slow tempo, and gradually get faster such as in the "Antidotum Tarantulae." The tarantellas from the Gargano section of Puglia, for instance "Alla Carpinese," are much softer and much slower, and accompanied on the chitarra battente (a 10 string strumming guitar, also the original metal string guitar from the 16th century, still popular today in southern Italy).

Pizzica: The form of the folk tarantella from the Salento region of Puglia, is the healing trance music and dance originally used during the therapeutic ceremonies. They are also played in 6/8, 12/8 and sometimes in 4/4. The pizzica is also a dance of courtship. The "Pizzica-Pizzica" is one of the oldest forms of the pizzica.

Neapolitan Villanella (16th Century): Polyphonic songs for two or more voices that were sung in the streets, piazzas, by the sea and in the taverns. They could be considered renaissance folk songs because of the text, written in Neapolitan dialect, almost always about love and were commonly used for the style of comic theater popular in Naples called *Commedia dell'Arte*. The rhythms vary quite often using cut time or have meter changes within the piece such as in " Vurria Addeventare," which goes from 4/4 into a 5/4 measure.

Tammurriata: Traditional song and dance from the region of Campania, based on the particular accents to the rhythms played on the large frame drum called the tammorra.

Lullabies: Used universally to put infants to sleep with a gentle repetitive rhythm and melody. Nonsense rhymes are commonly used, for instance *Bo e la ri- bo* and some text refer to the hardships in life.

Tarantella and Pizzica

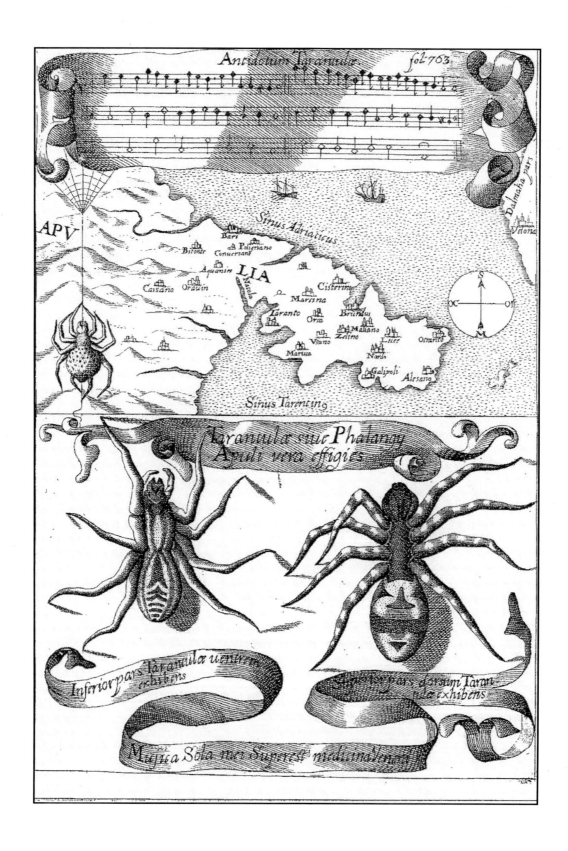

The tarantella exorcism ritual existed in Greece around the year 2000 BC and was connected to the divinities of Dionysus, Bacchus and Apollo (the Greek gods of eroticism, wine and music). It continued on in southern Italy, an area known as **Magna Grecia** (greater Greece).

In ancient times, in the Apuglia region of southern Italy, a type of spider known as *Lycosa Tarantula* was so prevalent, that it was named after the city of Taranto in that region. It was believed that the poisonous venom induced a hysterical condition followed by a sensation of melancholy, anguish, and depression. This illness became known as *Tarantism* or *Tarantulism*. The symptoms were also accompanied by an irresistible urge to dance in a wild and rapid whirling motion, to the point of exhaustion. This condition could only be suppressed and cured by very rhythmic and fast music, performed on specific instruments of high timbre, especially the violin, chitarra battente and the tambourine. Rites were performed to cleanse the body from demonic possession, a type of exorcism performed with music and dance. The music played for the cure became known as *Tarantella*. The *Pizzica*, which means, bite is the healing trance dance used to cure the victim. It is also known in Puglia as *morso d'amore*, or the " bite of love".

There have been many documents since the 1100's which speak about the relationship of musical exorcism for the poisonous bite of the tarantula. By the Middle Ages, a lot these beliefs were dismissed and suppressed by a new religion, more rational and austere and doctors supported the theory that diseases were provoked by natural causes and not by madness or diabolical possession. The adoration to the divinities of the past had ceased, but not forgotten. It was at this time that the myth of the "bite of the tarantula" was born.

During the 15th and 16th centuries, the illness was reaching epidemic proportions that bands of musicians roamed the countryside supplying the necessary music to cure the victims known as "tarantati". Fortunately, the Jesuit-Alchemist, Athanasius Kircher, who published a treatise on magnetism called *Magnes, Sive De Arte Magnetica Opus Tripartium*, notated some of these melodies. It was published in Rome in 1643. Kircher and other scientist of the day did not separate magic from science since magnetism was regarded as a magical force. He discusses various forms of magnetism, including the magnetic attraction of music and love. I have included some pieces transcribed from Kircher's famous treatise, including the antidote for the bite, and some of the tarantella's he also published in another treatise called *Phonurgia Nova*, Kempten.1673.

From ancient times till the present, this tradition has never ceased and is still very present in southern Italy. Called "Neo-Tarantismo" many young artists and famous musicians from the first revival of the 1970's are continuing to keep the tradition alive. Although the melodies are quite different from the examples we have from the 1600's, the rhythms and hypnotic effects are still the same. The constant repetition leads to trance and to a feeling of ecstasy. It's use to excersize a therapeutic action on certain forms of depression, hysteria and passion continues to be practiced and performed.

Pupi e Fresedde
One of the first groups reviving the pizzica traditions from Puglia.
A spontaneous street performance in Florence, Italy (ca.1976)
Dancers are Fulvio Sebastio and Pino De Vittorio. In the background
Angelo Savelli, and Tomasella Calvisi. Photo by Pier Paulo Alberti.

Italian Musical Expressions

Adagio......Slowly, leisurely
Accelerando (Accel.)......Gradually increasing the speed
Allegretto......Diminutive of allegro; moderately fast, lively
Allegro......Lively, brisk, rapid
Al Fine......To the end
Amoroso......Affectionately
Andante......In moderately slow tempo
Andantino......Diminutive of Andante, slower than Andante
A piacere......At pleasure
Arpeggio......Broken chord, harp style
A tempo......In the original tempo
Barcarolle......A boatman's song, popular in Naples and Venice
Cantabile......In a singing style
Coda......A supplement at the end of a composition
Con Moto......With motion, animated
Da or dal......From
Da Capo (D.C.)......From the beginning
Dal Segno (D.S.)......From the sign
Fine......The end
Grave......very slow and solemn
Larghetto......Slow, not as slow as Largo
Largo......Broad and slow, the slowest tempo mark
Legato......Smoothly, Tied together
Maestoso......Majestically, dignified
Meno Mosso......Less quickly
Moderato......Moderately
Mosso......Equivalent to rapid
Piacere,a......At pleasure
Piu`......More
Piu` Mosso......Quicker
Presto......Very Quick
Prestissimo......As quick as possible
Rallentando......Gradually slower
Ritardando......Gradually slower and slower
Staccato......Detached, separate
Tacit......Silent
Tempo......Movement, rate of speed.
Tempo primo......Return to the original tempo
Troppo......Too much
Veloce......Quick, rapid, swift
Vivace......With vivacity, bright, spirited
Vivo......Lively, spirited

The Tuning of the Mandolin

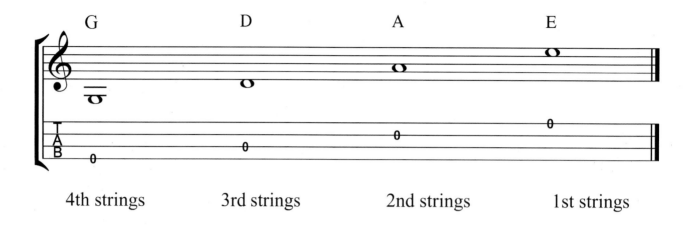

G   D   A   E

4th strings   3rd strings   2nd strings   1st strings

The mandolin and the violin share the same tuning, except the mandolin has four double strings.

Playing Position

If you decide to use a bowl back mandolin instead of the flat back, you will first find it a little more uncomfortable when you try to hold it and will require a little more attention. The mandolin can be played standing or sitting. In the seated position you must place the instrument on the right thigh supported by holding it close to the stomach and the right forearm. If it is held in the standing position, it is supported by the chest.

Sebastiano Passione and John T. La Barbera

14

Playing Techniques
The Position of the Pick and Right Hand

The right hand can be considered to be your paintbrush. To achieve the full expression of the music, it is necessary to have command of the pick in order to bring out the tone colors and dynamics on the instrument. The pick is held between the thumb and the first finger of the right hand. The other fingers of the right hand should be held close together under the thumb and first fingers. The forearm can lean on the side of the instrument with the side of the right hand wrist gently resting behind the bridge, holding the pick perpendicular to the strings. Play a downstroke with the pick hitting both strings evenly. Do not move the arm.

Once you feel comfortable holding the pick, you can begin to play expressively. First, practice playing *forte,* (loud) by holding the pick firmly and then play *piano,* (soft) by holding the pick lightly while plucking the strings between the edge of the sound hole and the bridge. Keep the wrist pressing down gently behind the bridge so that the pick can move according to the articulation in the music. With a slow steady beat play a down stroke immediately followed by an up stroke and then continue repeating until you have attained a quick and even movement keeping your wrist in the same position. It is important to move only the wrist, keeping the movements very concentrated and precise. This is called *tremolo.*

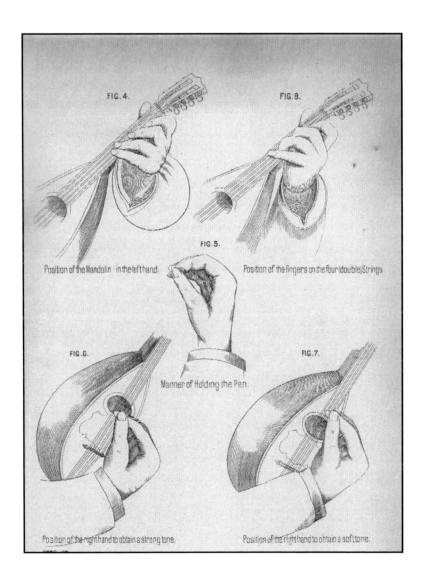

FIG. 4.　　　　　　FIG. 8.

FIG. 5.

Position of the Mandolin in the left hand.　　　Position of the fingers on the four (double) Strings

FIG. 6.　　　　　　FIG. 7.

Manner of Holding the Pen.

Position of the right hand to obtain a strong tone.　　　Position of the right hand to obtain a soft tone.

Tremolo

Always begin slowly with a downstroke of the pick followed by an upstroke, gradually increasing the speed. Eventually the tremolo should last the duration of the note value and is usually used to sustained notes.

The movements of the pick are indicated by two signs:

⊓ = the downstroke
∨ = the upstroke

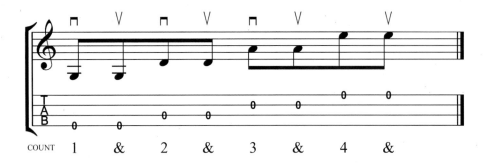

COUNT   1   &   2   &   3   &   4   &

double the pick strokes for the tremolo.   ♪ (sixteenth note).

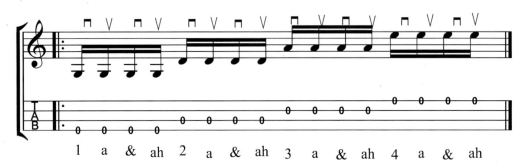

1   a   &   ah   2   a   &   ah   3   a   &   ah   4   a   &   ah

now play ⊓ and ∨ for each sixteenth note and you have thirty second notes.

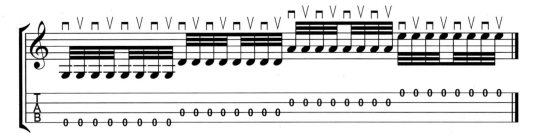

Tremolo is indicated by two diagonal slashes on the stem.
It can be played like the previous example.

The Left-Hand Position

The neck of the mandolin rests in the center of the left hand at the base of the index or the first finger, with the thumb close to the top of the neck. The fingers are placed perpendicular to the strings pressing down with only the tips of each finger against the fingerboard directly behind the fret. The fingers should be arched, keeping the last tip segment of the finger from collapsing. As a general rule, the fingering for the left hand is as follows:

    1st or 2nd fret-First finger
    3rd or 4th fret-Second finger
    5th or 6th fret-Third finger
    7th fret- Fourth finger

The fret numbers are indicated in the tablature.

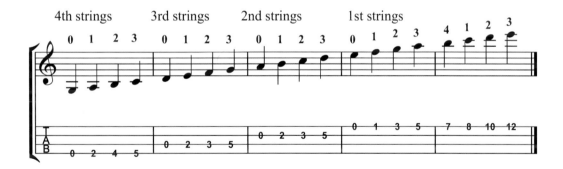

The Slur, Hammer-On and Pull-Off

The slur is a curved line drawn above or below a group of note of different pitches. It indicates that they are to be played legato (connected together without interruption between notes) with one pick stroke producing two notes. Use a downstroke to play a note on the second fret of the second string with the first finger of the left hand. Without plucking the string again, the second finger comes down on the next fret of the same string.

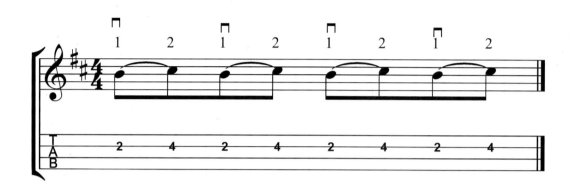

When a slur is played in an ascending direction it is called a *hammer-on*. The second finger is hammered down with a little more force. The finger tip must come straight down on the string. It is also possible to start on an open string. Try to play the first string open and hammer down on the second fret. Be sure to always use a down stroke.

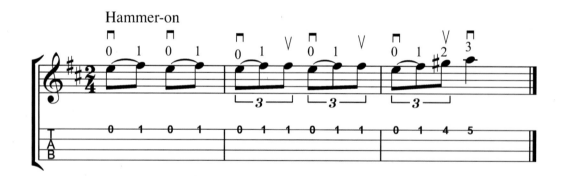

18

When the slur is played in a descending direction it is called a *pull-off* since the left-hand finger plucks the string.

The combination of these effects should contribute to more fluent phrasing once the left hand has achieved the proper strength.

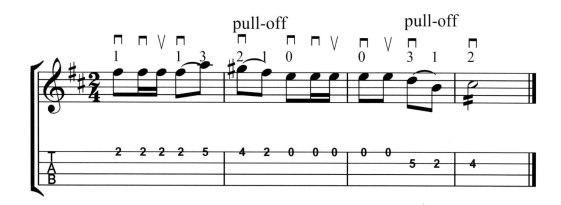

The Appogiatura or Grace Notes

The small notes placed before a principal one is called a *grace note* or an *appogiatura*. Grace notes have no set time value, but must be played very quickly before the principal note. It is always played with a down stroke on the small note as the left-hand finger pulls off the second second note.

Triplets

A triplet consists of three notes grouped together and played in the time value of two notes of the same value. It is usually indicated with the number 3 placed above or below the grouping and the notes are all played evenly. You can practice this by saying the the word "e-ven-ly" broken down into three syllables. When there is no accent on the notes and they are all found on the same string, the movement is always the same with the first note played with a down pick, followed by the up-stroke and the third note with the down pick.

In some instances when the triplet occurs on adjacent strings, the pick must glide over the strings playing all down pick, except when the second and third notes are repeated. The first note and second notes are down and the third one is an up stroke.

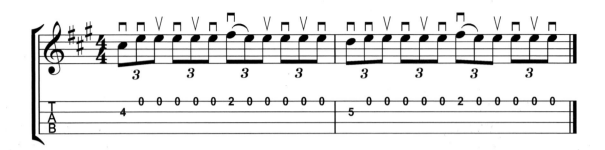

Sixteenth Notes

With sixteenth notes it is sometimes necessary to begin with a down pick and sometimes an up pick.When there is an even number of notes, you must begin with the downpick and then alternate each note. Also, if there is a pause after the first sixteenth note, you can use the downpick. Use the up pick when you begin on the second or fourth sixteenth note. Another exception is when you are playing rapid sixteenth notes on adjacent strings, you can use consecutive down picks as you cross strings.

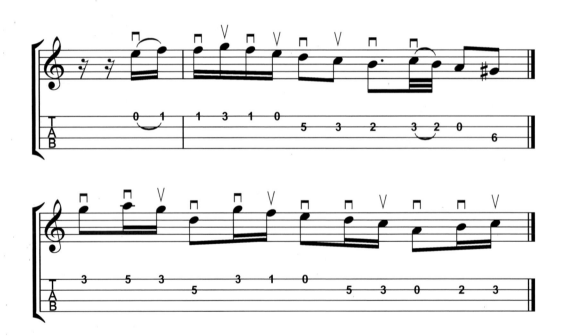

Rhythm Patterns for Accompaniment

With all of the songs in this book, I have included the chords to accompany them. Most of these chords are basic and can be played on mandolin or guitar, however the style of accompaniment and the rhythms are the two basic elements that distinguish this music. All of the up tempo dance music is always played with the traditional frame drums and or castanets. There are two principal types of frame drums. One is the *tamborello* (tambourine) used for tarantella and pizzica music and the other one is called the *tammorra*, (a larger drum with or without jingles on the rim) which is used for the *tammorriata*. The chordal accompaniment usually follows many of the same patterns as the percussion and is very rhythmic. The slower songs such as ballads, love laments, serenades and lullabies use a softer arpeggiated type of accompaniment.

Pizzica

The following accompaniment patterns are for the Pizzica rhythm and they should be played with the strum patterns indicated. These pieces are played quite fast and accompany the trance dances known as Pizzica-Tarantella. Most of the pieces are in compound time (6/8 or 12/8). When the music is in 4/4 you can still maintain the same pattern and accents as in the 12/8 time, for instance in Pizzicarella. It is written in 4/4, but the strum is the same as in 12/8. Pay close attention to the accents as well as the down and up strums. Repeat each section slowly until you can play it evenly. On the A chord, the accent falls on the 1st, and 3rd beat of the measure, followed by the E chord, with accents falling on the 1st, 2nd and 3rd beat. (1, 2, 123)

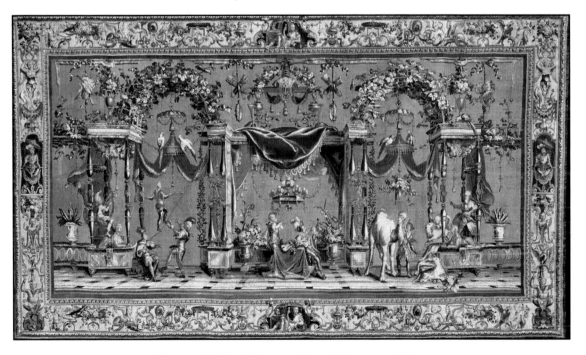

Image © The Metropolitan Museum of Art

This pattern continues throughout the piece with many variations.

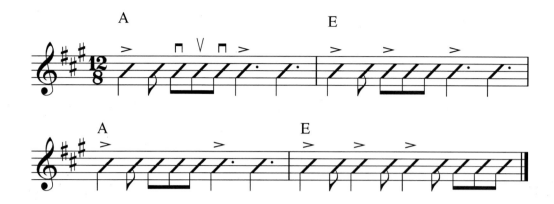

The accents remain the same while the variations change.

Variation 1:

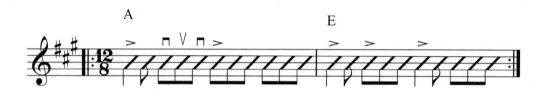

Variation 2 (triplets with repeated slur notes):

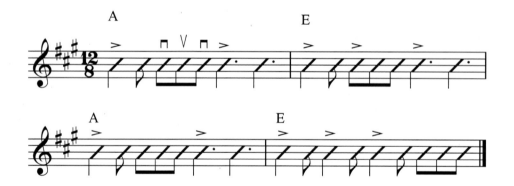

Variation 3 with closing phrase:

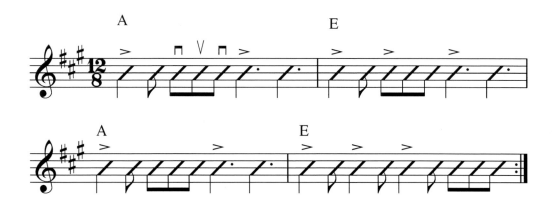

Tarantella

The basic rhythmic pulse for the tarantella in 6/8 time is found on accenting certain beats within a four bar phrase. Since 6/8 consists of 2 groups of triplets it is felt like two beats per measure. By accenting the first beat of the first measure, the first beat in the second measure, the first and second beat in the third measure and the first beat of the fourth measure, we arrive at the pattern that would be played as this (ex. from *Abballati, Abballati*.) Abballati, Abballati

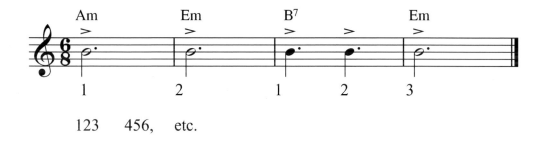

Strum followed by triplets. The accents are the same, but try to keep the triplets even. This pattern will work for many fast tarantellas.

(ex. *Tarantella dell'600*)

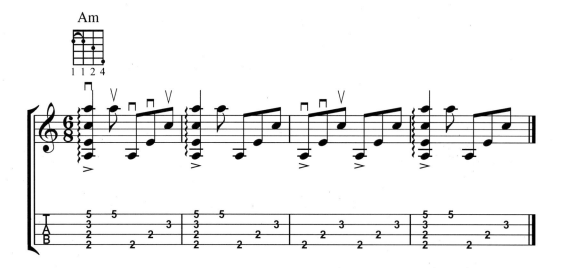

Tammurriata

Based on rhythms of the large frame drum called the *tammorra*. There are some slight variations. If there is a pickup measure, the pattern begins after the pickup and then remains constant. The accents fall on the first beat of the first, second and third measures, while the fourth measure has even eighth notes. This four bar pattern repeats within the piece.

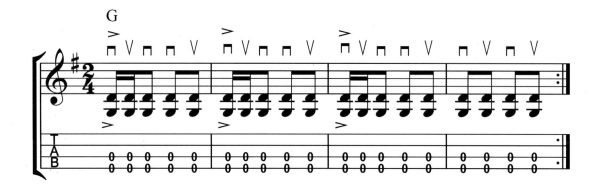

Arpeggiated Patterns

The arpeggiated patterns work well for the slower songs such as the lullabies, love songs and serenades. In order to create the harp like accompaniment the pick must glide evenly across the strings.

Variation1: this pattern uses three consecutive down picks (from low to high) and followed by three up picks (from high to low). Try to keep each note even and connected.
(ex. *Il Ritornello delle Lavandaie del Vomero*)

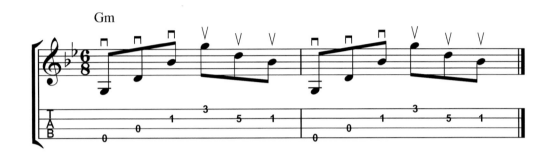

This arpeggio uses all down picking throughout the song with double notes occurring on the second beat of each measure. Try to maintain the steady pattern when the chord moves to (D7) on the second beat.
(ex. *La Procidana*).

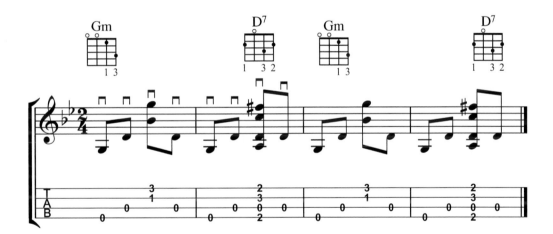

25

Track #1

Abballati, Abballati

Chiovu Abbalati, (song and dance) is a tarantella and one of the most popular pieces from the Sicilian tradition. This version comes from the 1800's however, many Sicilian songs are based on modes (which date back to it's ancient Greek influences) instead of tonality. Therefore, much of the music can be traced to older traditions. The song calls out: "get up and dance, there are so many beautiful women!"

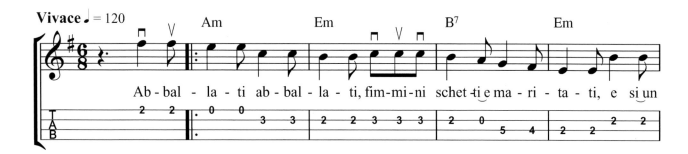

Ab - bal - la - ti ab - bal - la - ti, fim - mi - ni schet -ti e ma - ri - ta - ti, e si un

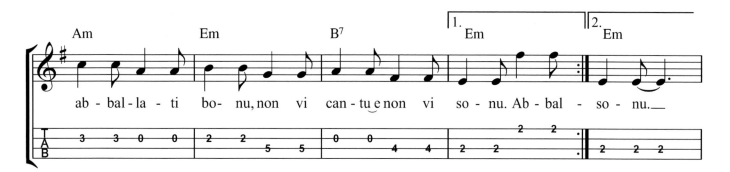

ab - bal - la - ti bo - nu, non vi can - tu e non vi so - nu. Ab - bal - so - nu.__

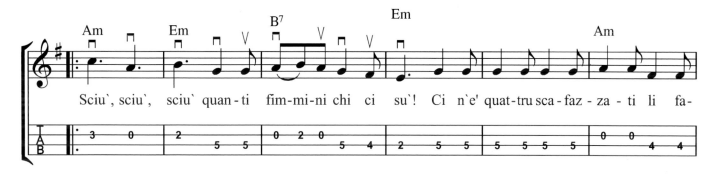

Sciu`, sciu`, sciu` quan - ti fim - mi - ni chi ci su`! Ci n`e' quat-tru sca-faz - za - ti li fa-

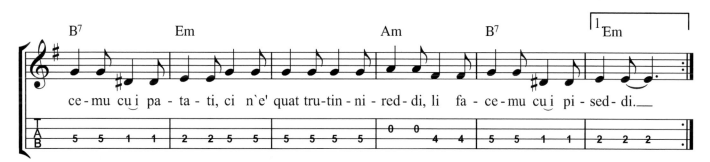

ce - mu cu i pa - ta - ti, ci n`e' quat tru-tin - ni - red - di, li fa - ce - mu cu i pi - sed - di.__

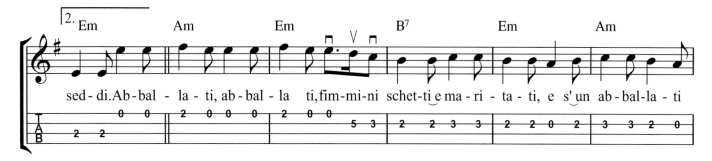

sed - di. Ab - bal - la - ti, ab - bal - la ti, fim - mi - ni schet-ti e ma - ri - ta - ti, e s' un ab - bal - la - ti

27

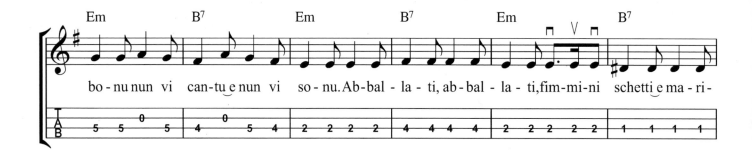

bo - nu nun vi can-tu e nun vi so - nu. Ab-bal - la - ti, ab - bal - la - ti,fim-mi-ni schetti e ma - ri-

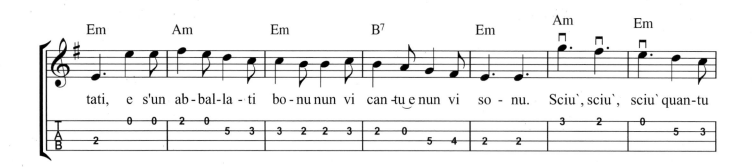

tati, e s'un ab-bal-la - ti bo-nu nun vi can - tu e nun vi so - nu. Sciù, sciù, sciù quan-tu

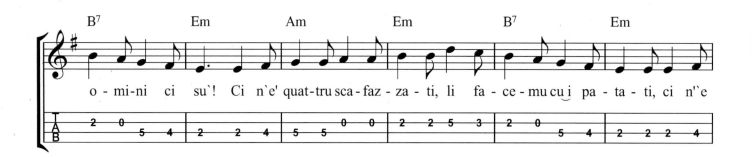

o - mi - ni ci su`! Ci n`e' quat-tru sca-faz-za-ti, li fa - ce-mu cu i pa - ta - ti, ci n'`e

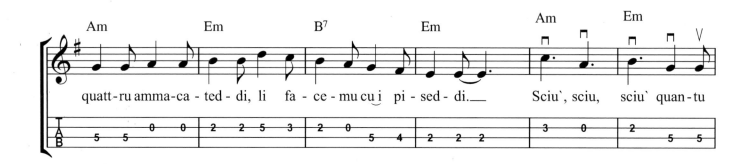

quatt-ru amma-ca-ted-di, li fa - ce-mu cu i pi-sed-di.__ Sciù, sciu, sciù quan-tu

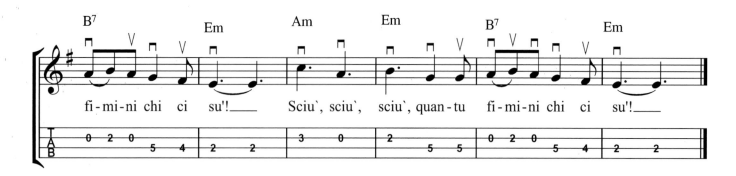

fi - mi-ni chi ci su'!__ Sciù, sciù, sciù, quan-tu fi-mi-ni chi ci su'!__

Alla Carpinese

This song is a shepherd's lament from Carpino, which is in the Gargano area of Puglia. Alla Carpinese means in the Carpino style and was usually played on the chitarra battente, an archaic steel string guitar from the sixteenth century, which the shepherds from this region have continually played. The opening melodic line descends chromatically until it settles into A minor. This version was recorded by Pupi e Fresedde on the album "La Terra del Rimorso".

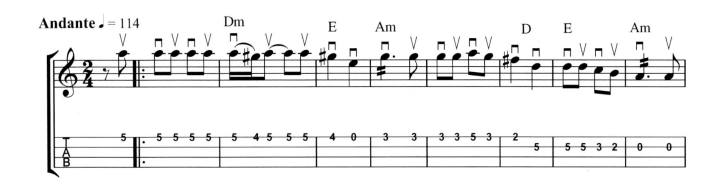

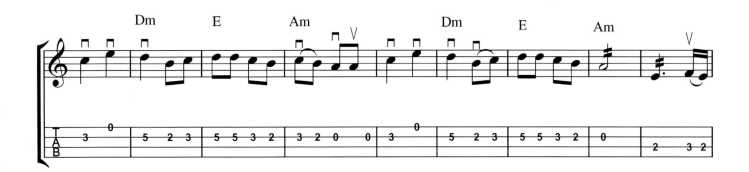

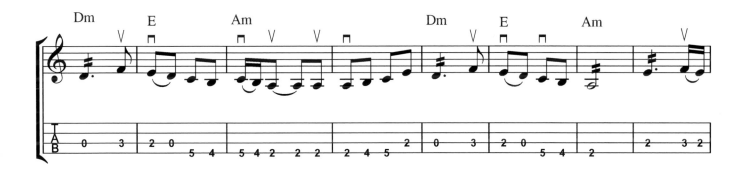

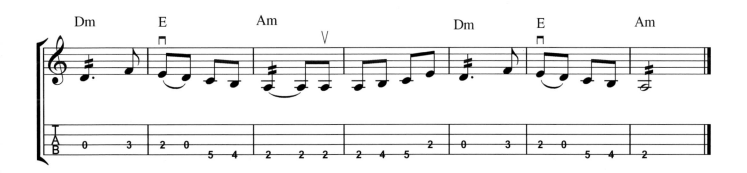

Alziti Bbella

This is a love serenade from the region of Lazio, near Rome. It calls the loved one to wake up and come to the window to be serenaded by this passionate love song. The first section has a laid back triplet feel to it with the tremolo only on the suggested beats.

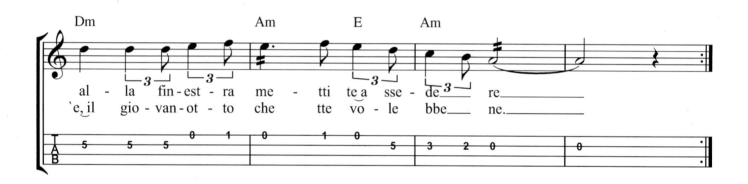

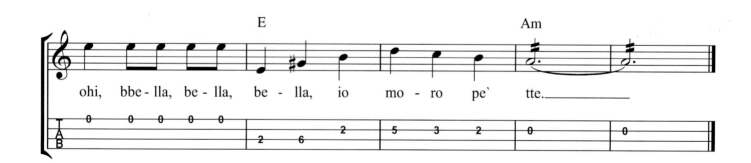

30

Angelare`

This song was popular in the islands of Procida and Capri, in the Bay of Naples, during the Eighteenth century. It's quieter softer sounds reflect most of the music from the fishermen in that area as opposed to music from the streets of Naples. It talks about one's longing for a love who has seemed to have vanished away mysteriously by a spell, cast by some magician or fairy. The music has a very hypnotic and dreamlike quality to it.

Lento ♩ = 60

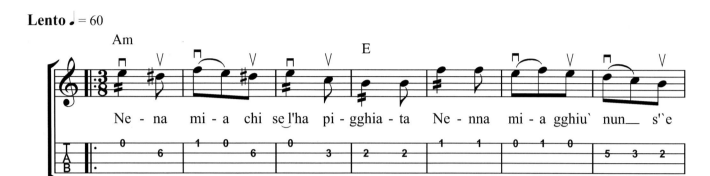

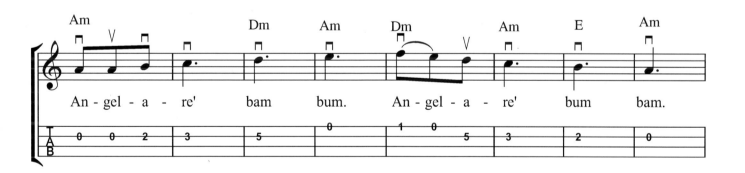

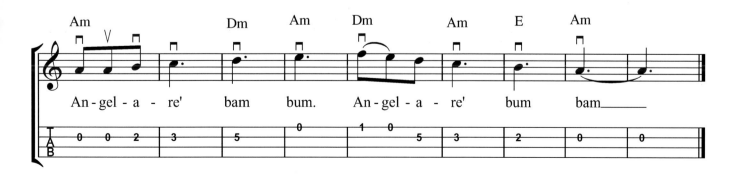

 Track #5

Antidotum Tarantulae

This is the "antidote" tarantella which was used in the healing rituals in Southern Italy. By the sixteenth and seventeenth centuries medical science was already studying the curing properties of the tarantella. This music was to put the victim in a calm trance-like state before or after dancing wildly to release the venom from the body. I have indicated the various sections which indicates the melodies used during the curing process and start slow and gradually progress faster. This melody was first transcribed by the Jesuit-alchemist Athanasius Kircher, in Phonurgia Nova (1673) Magnes sive de Arte Magnetica (1643).

Track #6

Antidotum Tarantulae (2nd part)

34

Bo e la ri-bo`

There are many variations on this popular lullaby from Sicily. "Go to sleep, your father will soon come home. He will bring you some little seeds, rosemary and basil." The words bo e la ri-bo`, is a nonsense rhyme popular in many Sicilian lullabies. It also means to fall asleep, or go back to sleep.

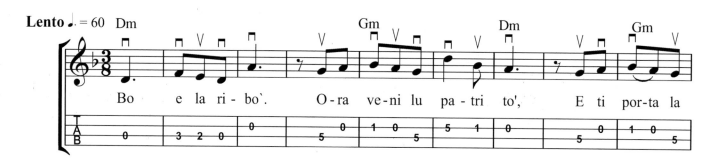

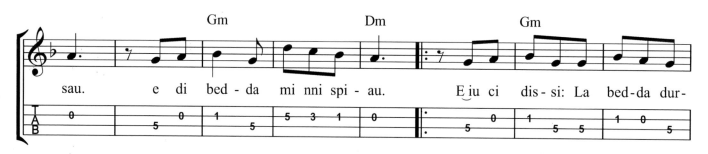

Cu Ti Lu Dissi

This is a Sicilian Mazurka. The mazurka is always in 3/4 time however the accent is always felt on the second beat (not the first like the waltz). The final phrases end with a short accent on the second beat followed by a rest on the third. Cu ti lu dissi means: who told you I didn't love you anymore? My heart sighs, you are the love of my life!

Danza Siciliano - "Jolla"

This is a typical Sicilian country dance that was popular in the late 1800's. Sicilian popular dances take on various names such as: quatrigghia, jolla, fasola, pasturale and of course tarantella. This shepherd's dance uses the binary form which goes from a major to minor key commonly found in the style of the "jolla".

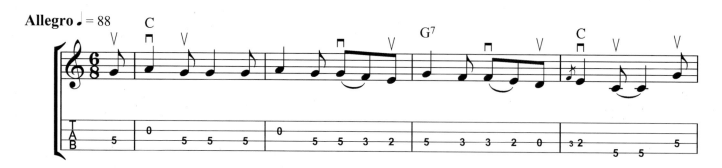

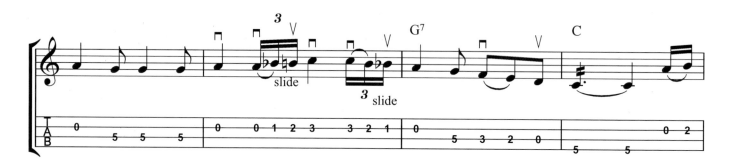

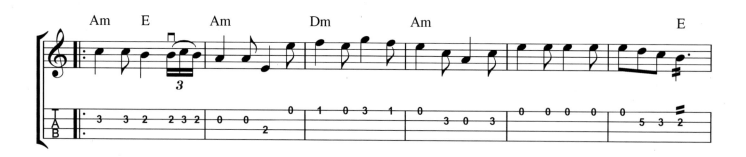

"Fasola" Siciliana

The Fasola, is a distincly popular Sicilian country dance. Salomone Marino, states in his 1897 edition of "Customs and Habits of the Sicilian Peasants", that the fasola may have been named for a 17th century musician of Palermo, a monk called Giovan Battista Fasola. It moves from the minor to relative major and ends in the parallel major key.

40

Figghia di'n Massaru
(The Almond Sorter's Song)

This is a narrative song from Sicily, which tells the tragic tale of the young daughter of a farm steward (massaru) who was condemned to death because she feared the loss of her inheritance upon her widowed father's remarriage. This song, recorded by Alan Lomax and Diego Carpitella during their field research in Italy in the 1950's, was sung by farm workers (almond sorters) to pass the time away. It appears on the Lomax collection of Sicilian traditional music, re-released on Rounder Records.

In pro - vin - cia_a Ca-tan-za ru____ 'na fa-mi gghia_ru - vi - na_ tu.____ u - na
o-ra spie- ggu_ lu mu-ti__ vo__ co-mu fu, 'ca__ co-min - ci au____ ques-tu

fi____ gghia, di'n ma - sa____ ru____ con-dan-na - ta_e poi_a mazz - a____ ta_____
fa____ ttu__ co - si vi__ vu,____ e cu fu, 'ca chi 'ncor - pau____

Fischiettando

"Fischettando" means whistling around. This type of country tarantella was commonly played on the Sicilian shepherd's flute (or whistle) called the "friscellettu".

Vivace ♩.=111

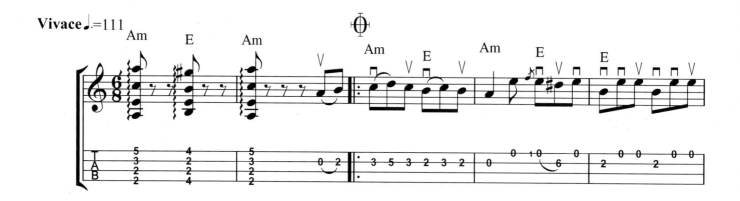

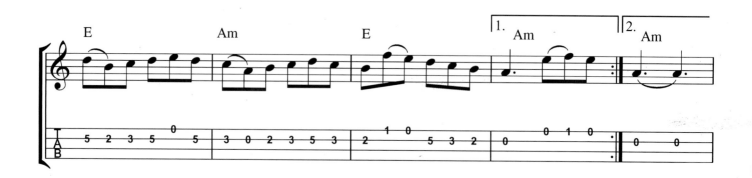

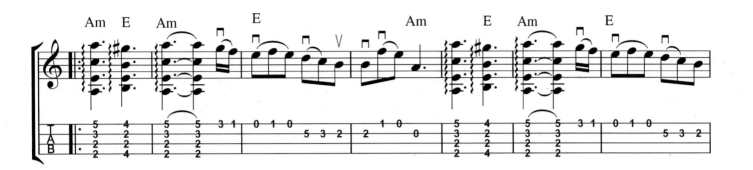

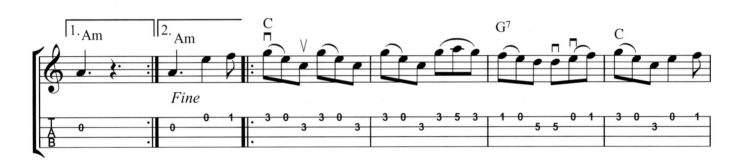

 Track #13

Fronni D'Alia

This is a ballad from the region of Basilicata which tells the story of three characters from medieval literature (1200). A young girl called Fronda d'Uliva is forced by her father to marry the rich Count Marco, but she loves Count Ruggerio. On her wedding night she plans to betray Marco and run to her true love. The slow melody was recorded by Alan Lomax during his field recordings of the 1950's and sung by olive pickers.

44

Il Ritornello delle Lavandaie del Vomero

This is an anonymous love song from the 14th century. It's title is translated as "The Song of the Washer-women of Vomero", (Vomero is a famous section in Naples). It was a popular tune which latter became known as a protest song against the foreign domination of the Aragonese (from Spain) in Naples. It was also known as "Lo Muccatura" which means handkerchief, however in this interpretation refers to the land that was being exploited.

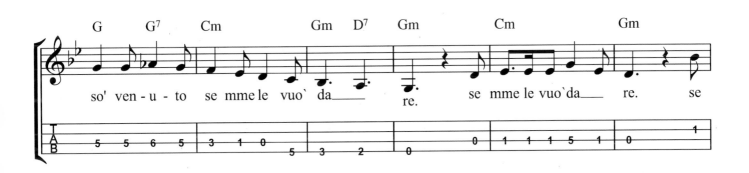

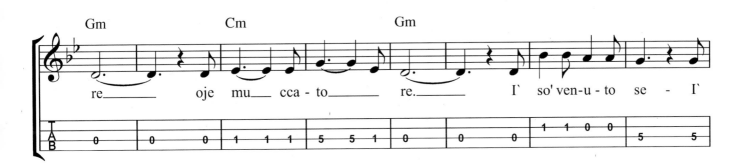

La `Ndrezzata

This is an ancient ritual song and sword dance done with a bastone (cane) from the island of Ischia in the bay of Naples. There are many legends about this music and dance, that go back to the ancient Greek god Apollo, who is credited for creating the first string instrument. It was believed that the nymph Corinide danced to this music while Apollo played his lyre. The use of the swords is believed to have originated with the soldiers of the legions of ancient Greeks who dominated the island in the 1st century B.C.

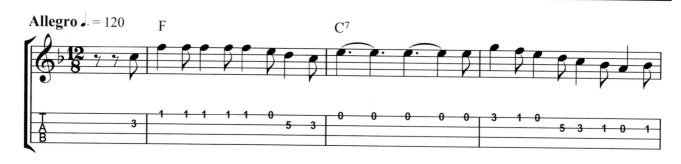

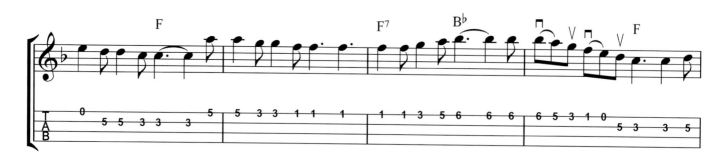

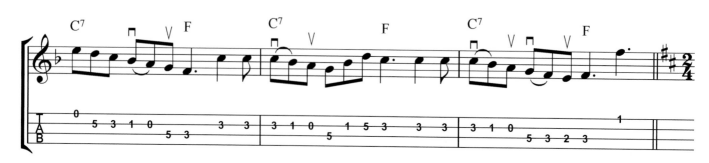

La Palumella

This is a love song from Naples. Palumella means "little dove" and the singer asks the dove to serve as a messsenger to find his love, who he believes has gone to paradise, and to tell her that he still sighs for her night and day. "If she is only sleeping send her my kisses".

Maestoso ♩ = 97

Pa - lu-mme - lla, zom-pa e vo - la ad- do` sta nen - nel__ la__ mi - a, non fer

mar - te pe la vi - a, vo - la, zom-pa a chel__ la__ la`. Co li

sce__lle la sa - lu__ ta, fal - le fe sta, fal-le fe-sta att -ourn-no att- uorno, e le

di`__che not-te e ghi-uorn-no io sto sem pre, io sto sem-pre a so-spi - ra`!

La Procidana

This is a fisherman's love serenade from the island of Procida in the Bay of Naples. Simlilar to the Barcarole, which are usually in 6/8 rhythm, and imitates the soothing rowing motions, the fisherman's songs were inspired by the sea and the woman they love.

quant'-e' bel-la - l'a-ri-a, O quant'-e' bel-la - l'a-ri-a - l'a-ri-a de lu Ma - re.
sta 'na fi - gli-a de, - c'e sta 'na fi - gli-a de, - de lu ma - ri - na - ro.

Nu me ne di - ce oi co - re tu me ne di - ce oi co - re de par - ti -
Tan-te ch'e' bel - la - che - tan-te ch'e'bel - la che - mi fa mu - ri -

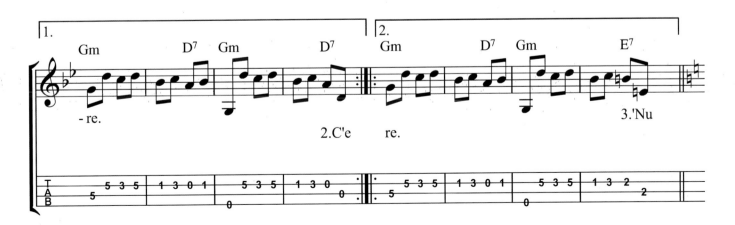

- re.   2.C'e   re.
                                                          3.'Nu

49

La Sant' Allegrezza

This is a Neapolitan Christmas song played in the style of the "zampognari", (shepherds who play the traditional Italian bagpipes and come down from the mountains during Christmas time). They stroll thru the steets playing these pastoral melodies as they have for centuries.The chord voicings imitate the sound of the bagpipe drones.

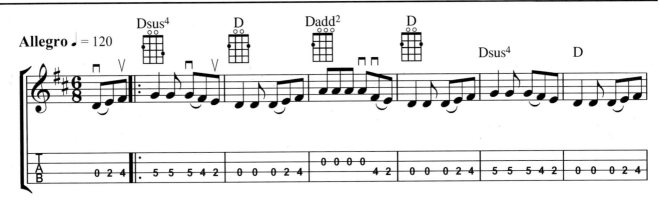

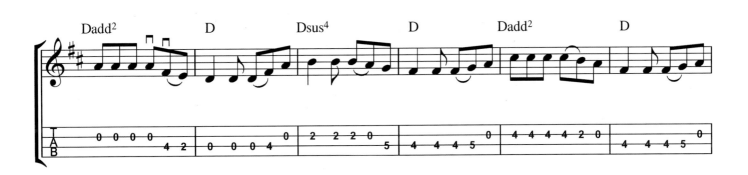

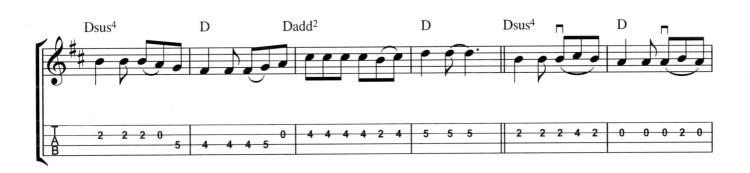

51

La Zita Passa

From Puglia, this piece is translated as "The Bride Passes". While I was living in Italy I had learned this song from Pupi e Fresedde who originally heard a young girl singing this nonesense rhyme in the streets as she was playing. The song talks about a young bride (la zita) who is married off by her family against her wishes and the hardships she must endure. It is played with a tarantella beat.

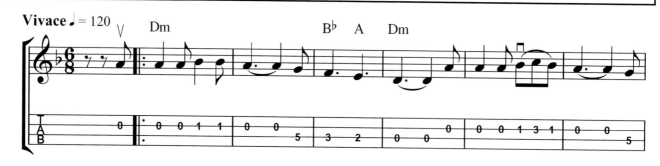

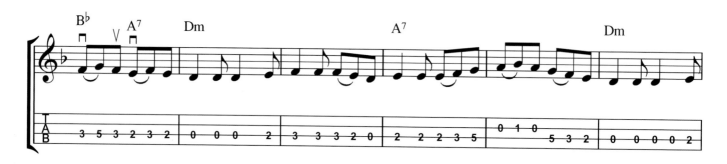

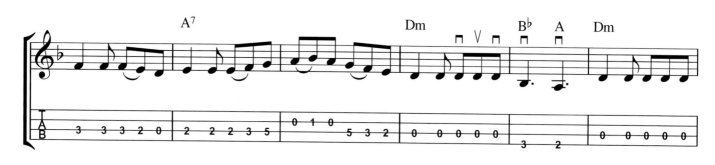

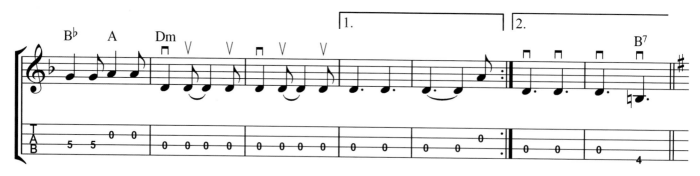

52

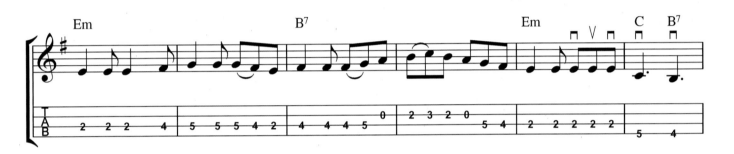

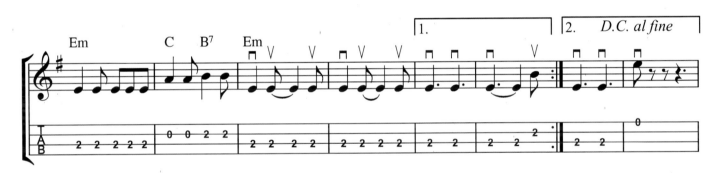

Track #20

Marenaresca

This is a fisherman's serenade from the Bay of Naples, dating back to the 18th century. Similar to the Venetian Barcarole, boatmen (called barcarolo in Italian) had a tradition of singing love songs as they row. The accompaniment usually suggested the steady rhythm of the oars.

54

Matajola

This is a courtship song from Calabria. This arrangement is written as a duet between two lovers.
The chords and rhythm should sound very laid back, with a blues feeling. The melody itself has this quality
for example the G natural against the E7 chord creates a #9th, which is very common in jazz music.

55

Motivo di Cantastorie

The title for this piece is called the "Theme of the Storyteller" from Palermo, Sicily. It was originally transcribed by the Sicilian composer-musicologist Alberto Favara during the early 1900's. He had learned it from a railroad capitan of the Steam Locomotive. Similar melodies like this were once used to sing the stories of the Brigante (bandits) who roamed thru Southern Italy during the late nineteenth century.

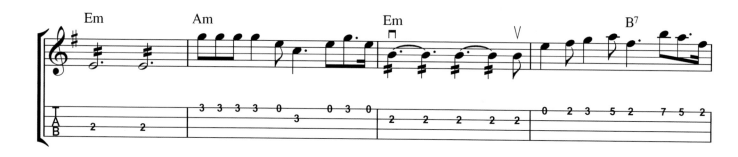

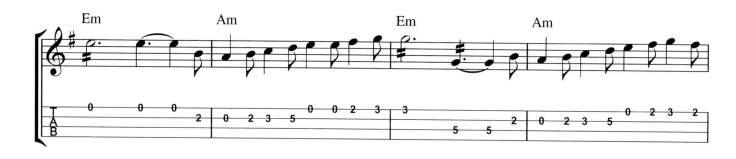

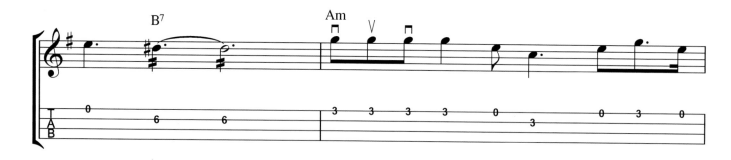

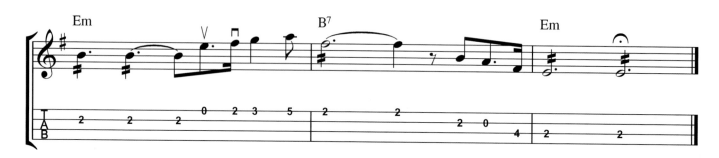

Pizzicarella Mia

This is probably one of the best known Pizzica's from the Salento region in Pugia. It is a "pizzica da cuore", (pizzica of love) and talks about the admiration one has for his "Pizzicarella", an affectionate term for young lovers and who's way of walking seems like a dance. It is played a little slower than most Pizzica's and less frenetic.

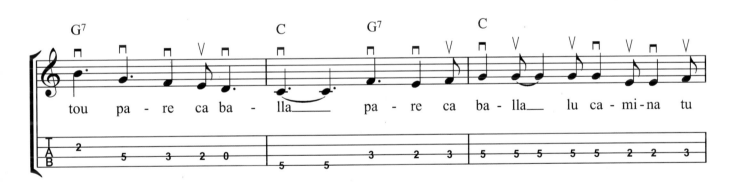

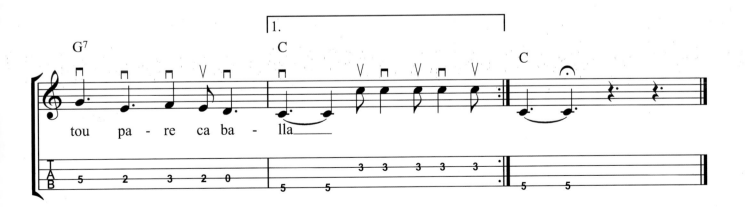

Pizzica-Pizzica

Pizzica-Pizzica, means the "bite", or the sting of the tarantulla. It is a form of tarantella from the Salento region in Puglia where this piece is from and it's rhythm has a distinct character different from tarantellas from other parts of southern Italy.

58

Pizzicarella

This Pizzica is from the Salento region of Puglia. It begins with a very slow introduction, without rhythmic accompaniment, in the style of the tarantellas of the Middle ages that were used for the healing rituals. It keeps the slow hypnotic melody until it goes into the frenetic dance which is always sung with lyrics pertaining to love.

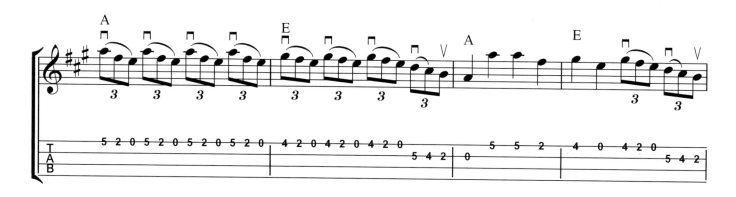

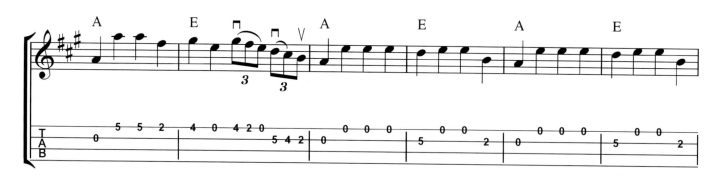

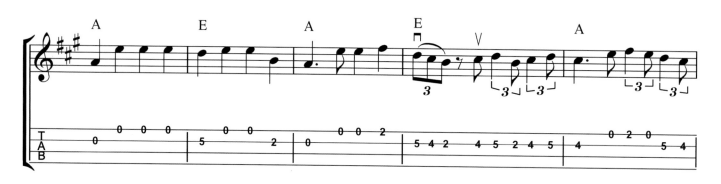

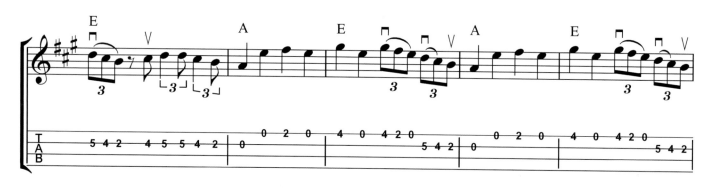

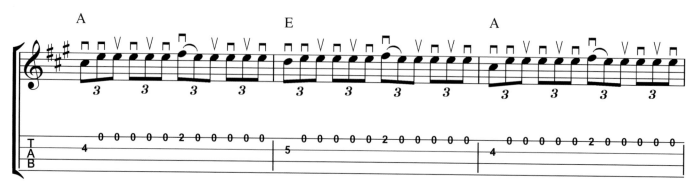

61

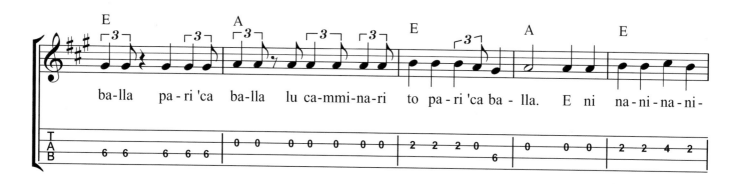

ba-lla   pa - ri 'ca   ba-lla   lu ca-mmi-na-ri   to pa - ri 'ca ba - lla.   E ni   na - ni - na - ni-

na   be-ddu l'a - mo - re   ci   lu sa-pi   fa.   E ni   na - ni - na - ni - na   be-ddu -l'a

1.2.

D.S. al coda

mo - re   ci   lu sa-pi   fa.

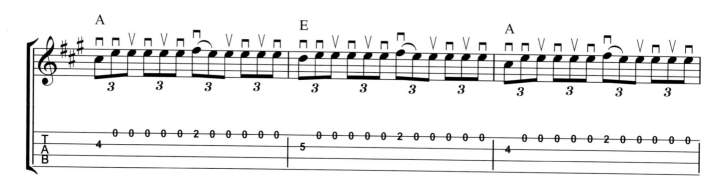

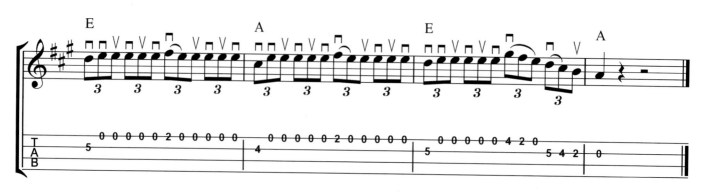

Track #26

Ricciulina

This is a Neapolitan villanella (a form of folksong from Naples) from the sixteenth century. The villanella form usually had three part harmonies with the lyrics written in the local Neapolitan dialect. It was often used in staged performances of the commedia dell'arte. Ricciulina means "girl with curly hair". Commedia dell'Arte was the first style of theater that had female stock character on stage. Ricciulina was one of them. It can be played as a duet.

63

Serenata Amalfitana

This Serenade, is attributed to the composer Guillaume L. Cottrau (1797-1847). The text, in Neapolitan dialect, is about a woman, who is haunted by the restless spirit of her lover who keeps returning back to her in a dream, and she feels tormented and can't sleep.

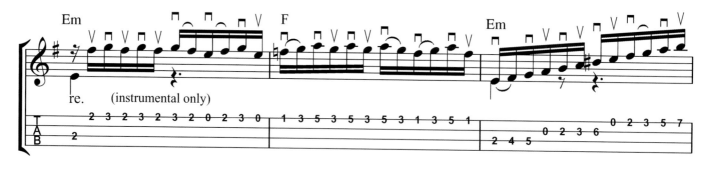

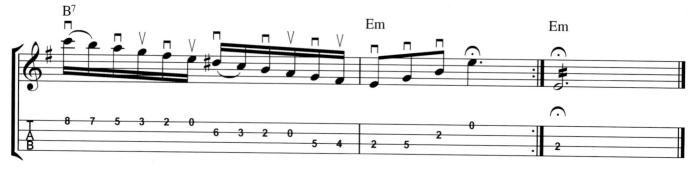

Sonos `E Memoria

This piece entitled "Sounds of Memory", is a traditional Sardinian love ballad. I learned this from one of Italy's most famous female vocalists of folk music, Maria Carta. We performed it together on our American tour, in 1986. It is also the title of her Album on the Fonit-Cetra Album (CIS 1001). Maria Carta, represented the soul of Sardinian culture.

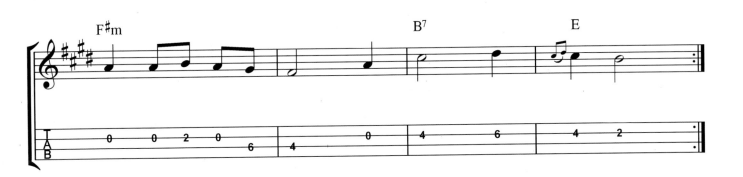

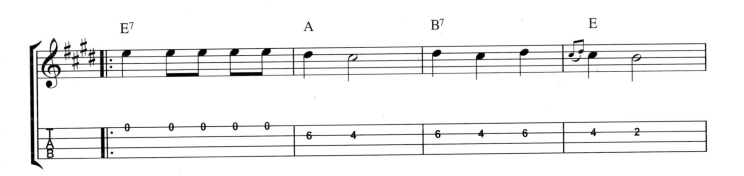

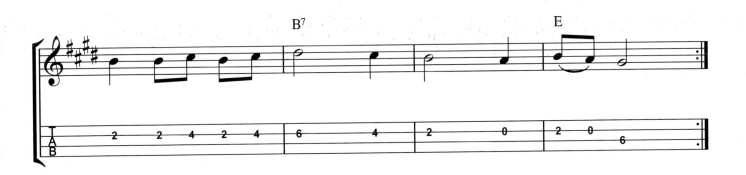

Tammurriata

 Track #29

The tammuriata is a traditional dance as well as a particular rhythm style which derives from the large frame drum called the "Tammorra". It is very popular in Naples and the region of Campania . The melody is derived from achaic melodic styles using the lydian mode (raised 4th degree of the major scale) with improvisational lyrics under the repeated rhythmic cycle. You can try to play this melody together with the open G and D strings playing the rhythmic drone.

66

Tarantella 'Nfuocata

This is called "The Inflammed, or Red-Hot" tarantella from Calabria. It has a very slow introduction similar to the archaic pizzica's from Puglia, which can be very rubato. Most of the piece is in A minor except for a short passage into G major. The dance to this piece is just as passionate as the music and swirls into a trance like frenzy till the end. It has to be played "hot".

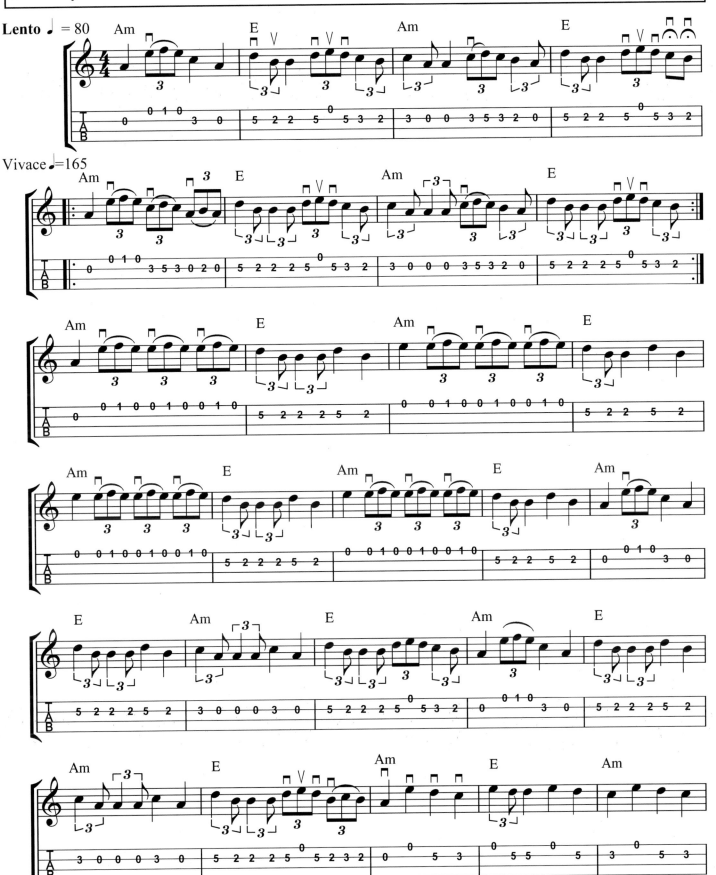

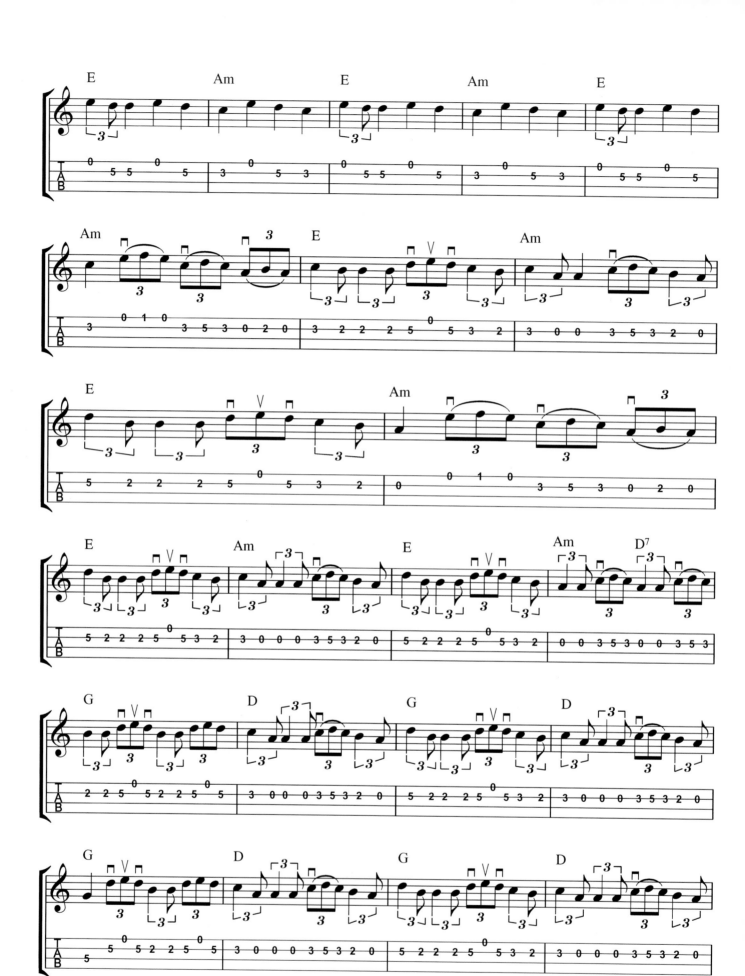

 Track #31

Tarantella di Ogliastro

This tarantella is from the town called Ogliastro (olive branch), which is in the region of Campania. It is an "excorsism" tarantella played to cast away the "malocchio", or evil eye. It's form consists of a theme, found in the first four bars of the melody, with variations or improvisations. It alternates between theme and variation and ends on the theme again.

71

Tarantella dell '600

This tarantella is from the 1600's and has three different sections which repeat until the final coda. It's origins are probably from Puglia, however it appears in an anonymous manuscript of: "Piezas para Clave", found in the Biblioteca Nacional de Madrid. (MS.M 1250 Fondo Barbieri).

Tarantella Paesana

This is a Sicilian tarantella "alla paesana", which means from the rural countryside. It's form is a little bit different from most tarantellas. After the intro, it picks up tempo in the minor key (A minor) then moves to the parallel major (A major) after repeating the minor theme again it then moves to the relative major key (C major) and finally ends again back in minor.

73

Villanella Ch' All'Aqua Vai

This is an anonymous Neapolitan villanella from the sixteenth century. The most important subject of the villanella is love. Villanella also means a young woman from the countryside. "Villanella, who goes to the water, I am dying for you and you don't know it. When you go to the water you are a Queen not a peasant. Alas, I die thinking of you." This piece clearly has elements of renaissance folk music with the simplicity of the melody and the rural setting of the poetry.

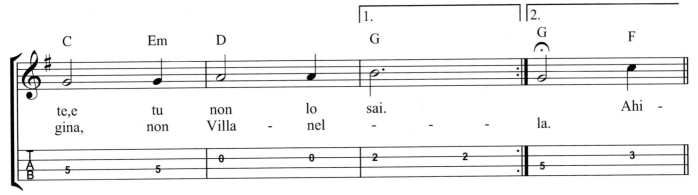

Volumbrella

This piece is from the region of Campania, near Naples. This popular melody is similar to early monophonic thirteenth century song. Volumbrella refers to a fig or a fig tree in southern Italy. It has a short melody which is repeated an octave higher for variation.

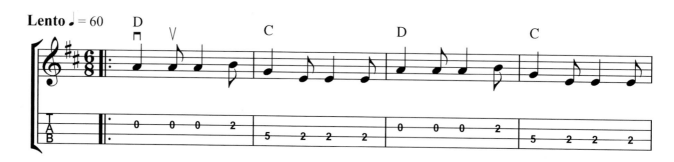

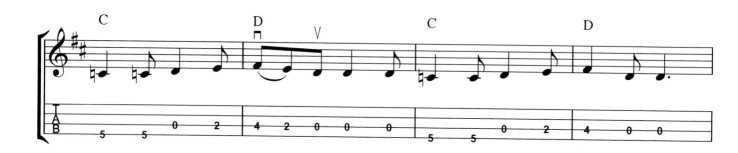

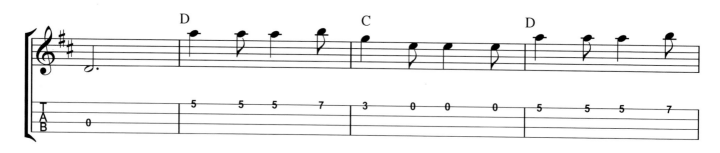

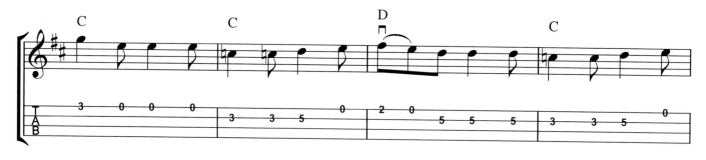

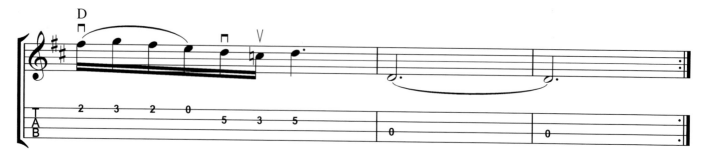

Vurria Addeventare

This is a 16th century Neapolitan villanella credited to Gian Leonardo dell'Arpa (1520-1602). The text is written in the Neapolitan dialect. "Vurria Addeventare", (I would like to become), is an amourous expression which expresses the desire to become an object very dear to his/her loved one so that they could stay close by at all time. The tempo remains the same during the 5/4 measure.

Chord Dictionary

MAJOR CHORDS

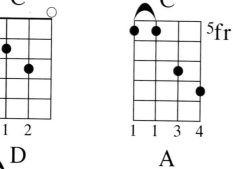

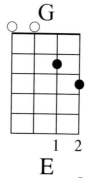

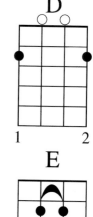

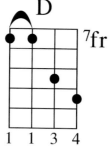

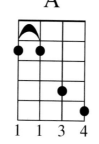

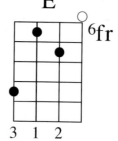

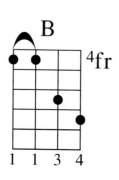

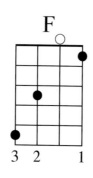

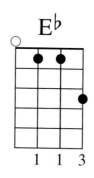

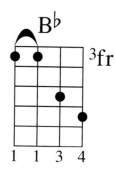

MINOR CHORDS

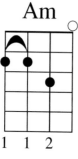

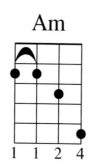

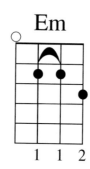

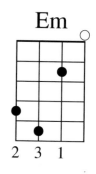

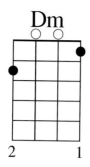

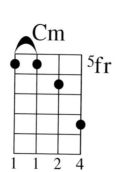

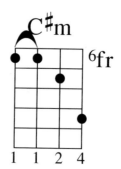

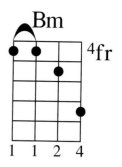

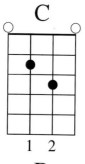

78

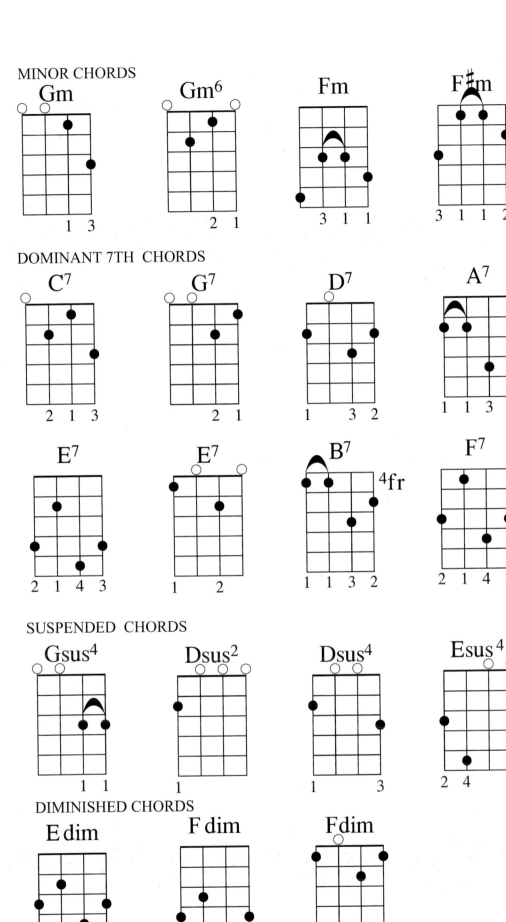

MINOR CHORDS

DOMINANT 7TH CHORDS

SUSPENDED CHORDS

DIMINISHED CHORDS

About the Author

John T. La Barbera

For more than three decades, guitarist, mandolinist, and composer arranger, John T. La Barbera, has enchanted audiences throughout the United States, Europe and South America.

He was awarded for the extraordinary role of the transmission and translation of Italian oral traditions from **The Italian Oral History Institute** in 2005 and recognized as one of the first transcribers of Southern Italian folk music in America.

Immediately after graduating with a Bachelor of Music degree in classical guitar from the **Hartt School of Music** in Hartford, Connecticut, he was awarded a scholarship to continue graduate studies in Siena and Florence, Italy. It was in Florence during the 1970's where John launched his professional career. It was his selection as full time guitarist and arranger for the music and theater company **Pupi e Fresedde**, that honored his virtuosity and brought him acclaim in Italy and the rest of Europe. During these years, the group left an indelible mark and vast contribution to folk music in Italy. It was also when he started to transcribe a huge repertoire that had been passed down by oral tradition. Upon his return to the U.S., he brought back his experience and own transcriptions of this music to form **I Giullari di Piazza**, in New York City in 1979.

As a composer, La Barbera has won several awards and commissions. From The Jerome Foundation he was commissioned to write a work for the ETHOS Percussion ensemble, *The Marimba Suite* for percussion, which premiered in 2001 and released on their CD Sol Tunnels; in 1996 by Lincoln Center for the Performing Arts, The Martin Gruss Foundation and the New York State Council on the Arts in New York, to compose *The Dance of the Ancient Spider,* which premiered at Alice Tully Hall; Funding from the New York State Council on the Arts and meet the Composer; commissioned by the Cathedral of Saint John the Divine in New York City to compose *Stabat Mater-Donna Di Paradiso*; numerous composer awards from ASCAP and finalist in the John Lennon Songwriting Competion.

Because of his expertise in Italian traditional music, LaBarbera has been a valuable resource for both film and theater directors. His film scores often include mandolin as the principal instrument, as in the Acadamey Award Nominated feature documentary: *Children of Fate*, (1992), *Sacco and Vanzetti* (2007); *Pane Amaro* (2007); and *La Festa* (1996) and *Tarantella* (1994). Other films include: *What's up Scarlet* (2005) and *Cuore Napolitano* (2000).

In Theater, his expertise as composer, arranger and musical director was valuable in the off-Broadway productions of *Souls of Naples*, 2003, (Theater for a New Audience) starring John Turturro (Miller's Crossing, Barton Fink) and the stage adaptation of Sicilian playwright Luigi Pirandello's short stories in *Kaos*, 2006 (New York Theater Workshop) directed by Marta Clarke.

Composer of original Folk Operas:
Stabat Mater: Donna di Paradiso 1995
The Voyage of the Black Madonna 1990
The Dance of the Ancient Spider 1996
La Cantata dei Pastori
La Lupa- the She-Wolf 1987
The Adventures of Don Giovanni and His Servant Pulcinella 1987

As founder and musical director of **I Giullari di Piazza** since 1979, together with singer/percussionist Alessandra Belloni, the group has presented legendary folk operas and hypnotic music and dramatic stories to the delight of audiences around the US. They are also "artists in residence" at the New York City's Cathedral of St. John the Divine at the Caramoor Center for Music and the Arts, in Katonah, New York.

La Barbera performs regularly in concert halls around the world including: the Montreal Jazz Festival, Carnegie Hall, Symphony Space, Lincoln Center, UCLA, the San Franciso World Music Festival, the World Music Institute, and throughout Brazil.

He holds a B.M. from the Hartt School of Music, (Univ.of Hartford), with graduate courses at William Paterson University, Hunter College in ethnomusicology, in Italy at the Villa Schifanoia (Rosary College), in Florence and in Siena, at the Accademia Chigiana's film music seminar with Ennio Morricone.

He currently teaches at the Bergen Community College in Paramus, New Jersey and has taught at The Julius Hartt School of Music (University of Hartford); The Guitar Study Center of the New School in N.Y.; Sessione Sienese in Siena, Italy; SASI in Bratislava, Slovakia; and SESC in Sao Paulo, Brazil. He conducts workshops and lectures on mandolin and acoustic guitar styles, ethnomusicology, world music, and has written for Acoustic Guitar magazine. His music has been recorded on Shanachie records, Meadowlark, Rounder Records, Lyrichord Disks, Ellipsis Arts, and Bribie records.

Participation on Recordings of Traditional Southern Italian Folk Music:

La Terra del Rimorso-Pupi e Fresedde, (Divergo-Polygram) DVAP 029, Milano-Italy
*Addo t'ha Pizzicato la Tarantella- (I Giullari di Piazza)
*Sullilo Mio- I Giullari di Piazza, Meadowlark Records (Shanachie) Meadowlark 106
*Dea Fortuna- I Giullari di Piazza, (Shanachie Records)-21010
*Cantata dei Pastori- I Giullari Productions
*Earth, Sun and Moon- I Giullari di Piazza, (Lyrichord Discs) LYRCD 7427
*String Ecstasies-   John La Barbera (SESC) Live concert in Brazil
*In The Labyrinth- John La Barbera (Itri Music)
*Global Celebrations- (Ellipsis Arts) 3230
*Mediterranean Lullabies- Various artists (Ellipsis Arts) 4290
*Papa's Lullabies- Various artists (Ellipsis Arts) 4292
*Mother Earth Lullabies- Various artist (Ellipsis Arts) 4293
*Tarantata-Dance of the Ancient Spider- Alessandra Belloni, (Sounds True) STA MM00117D
*Tarantelle & Canti d'Amore- Alessandra Belloni, (NaxosWorld)76049-2
(* = composer-arranger-producer-multi-instrumentalist)

Reviews:
"The ensemble led by John La Barbera, Musical Director, produced non-stop theatrical and musical energy".
N.Y. Times, Alex Ross

"The music, directed by John La Barbera is folkish aiming for vitality above precision and often achieving both".
New York Times, John Pareles

"John LaBarbera, kicks things into overdrive with his hand-driving contributions on oud, mandocello and guitar.."
Pulse Magazine, -J.Poet,

"La Barbera fitted all of this (Stabat Mater) out with a kicky new score...it was slickly produced and smoothly executed...his 4 part setting of the ancient Stabat Mater text made for a touching light motif".
New York Times, James Oestreich

" Mr. LaBarbera's "Marimbaba Suite" was a set of three cheerful homages to Brazilian folk music: bouncy, dreamy and bouncy again... this was music you wanted to be dancing to...
New York Times, Paul Griffiths.

"This CD (Earth, Sun, And Moon) is highly recommended for a powerful blend of traditional rhythms, instruments and themes from various ages and cultures".
Rhythm Music Magazine

"..John's immense knowledge of traditional Italian music was a great asset to the production. It gave his original compositions a feeling of authenticity that supported the story of the film.." (Children of Fate).
Archipelago Films. Andrew L. Young, Director

"John La Barbera's stunning compositions and phenomenal playing, along with the entire ensemble's spirited performance, put this recording in a class by itself".
Lyrichord Discs

"John La Barbera's original music marks him as a contemporary Kurt Weill."
Backstage.com, Victor Gluck

"The momentum builds to a pitch in both acts thanks to the haunting and feverish score by John La Barbera".
Village Voice, Robert Massa

"Congratulations on the wonderful work created by John La Barbera".
Lincoln Center for the Performing Arts, Jenneth Webster, producer

"...Stabat Mater is one of the best productions at the Cathedral in the last 23 years".
The Very Reverend Dean James Parks Morton, former Dean of the Cathedral of St. John the Divine, NYC.

'...The production values are high... and the striking use of music, and a haunting score, were composed and performed by John La Barbera".
The Herald, Edinburgh, Scotland

'...John La Barbera is North American born with the dance of music in his fingertips. His articulations on either instrument, intimate and classically fine, are filled with the light of a born Latino".
Woodstock Times

" The Collection of Songs on In The Labyrinth will carry you across several continents as guitarist John La Barbera rightfully proclaims his virtuosity."
to the bone.com, Tracy Romoser

Bibliography

Chiriatti, L. (1997). *Morso d'Amore:Viaggio nel tarantismo salentino*. Lecce: Capone Editore.

Cannistraro, P.V. (Ed.). (1999). *The Italians of New York*: *Five Centuries of Struggle and Acheivement*. New York: The New York Historical Society and The John D. Calandra Italian American Institute.

Carpitella, D. & Lomax, A. (Compiled and Edited). (1955).
The Columbia World Library of Folk and Primitive Music: Volume XVI Southern Italy. (Record album No. 91A 02025). Columbia Records.

Del Giudice, L. (Ed.). (1995). *Italian Traditional Song*. (audio cassette recording). Los Angeles: Istituto Italiano di Cultura.

Pianagua-Rodriguez, G. (Director). (1978). *The Tarantula*. Recorded by Atrium Musicae de Madrid. (Record Album No. 4050). Evenston, Illinois: HNH Records.

Sparks, P. (1995). *The Classical Mandolin*. Oxford: Clarendon Press.

Sparks, P. , & Tyler, J. (1989). *The Early Mandolin*. Oxford: Clarendon Press

Contact information:
John T. LaBarbera
e-mail:labmambo@aol.com;
www.johntlabarbera.com; www.myspace.com/johntlabarbera

for traditional Italian mandolins:
Musikalia-Dott. Alfio Leone-Catania, Sicily. www.musikalia.it